The Incredible Journey

Written by Frank Pedersen
Illustrated by Robert Mancini

Contents

Meet the Characters

Sambula

A young African soldier.

Luiz

A poor Brazilian.

Rihanna

An American girl.

An Old Man

An African statesman.

Also Featuring

Mandawuy

An Australian fisherman.

Dear Reader

We all share the same world – and every one of us is connected to each other. In this book, I wanted to tell the story of some people who never met but who were connected by something special, and whose lives were changed by the thoughts that they shared. I hope you enjoy it – and pass on the story to someone else!

Frank Pedersen

Author

The Incredible Journey

1. Africa to Brazil
2. Brazil to the USA
3. The USA to Australia
4. Australia
5. Australia to Africa

1 The Journey Begins

Above the thunderous crash of the waves on the deserted, moonlit African shore, the crackle of gunfire and the flat thump of explosions woke Sambula.

He sat up, instantly alert, his heart pounding. Through the darkness, there was another burst of gunfire – but Sambula breathed a sigh of relief. It was far off in the distance. Then the pain in his leg returned, a dull throbbing ache that brought back some terrible memories.

When the rebel soldiers had come to his village, they had gathered all the young boys together. The life of a child soldier, they had said, was one of adventure and endless excitement. Imagine how exciting it would be to fire real bullets from real guns. Imagine the freedom of having no rules.

The rebel soldiers smiled a lot. But all Sambula could think of was an old proverb his grandfather had once told him: "If you can see the teeth of a lion, he may not be smiling at you."

Sambula knew he had no choice. Behind their smiles, the rebel soldiers had hard, dangerous faces. If he refused to join them, terrible things might happen to his village. He went with the soldiers.

Later that fateful afternoon, on the dry, dusty road north, the rebel truck full of soldiers and children had struck a landmine.

Flung from the tangled wreckage, Sambula had been lucky to escape with only an injured left leg. After a few weeks, he was able to walk again. But late at night, the pain – and the memory of the terrible explosion – often kept him awake.

Sambula silently slipped past the sleeping sentries, and walked quietly down to the beach. From his belt, he drew the sharp knife that he always carried with him – and from the pocket of his tattered army shirt, he carefully took out a piece of wood.

The small, carved boat that he had been slowly shaping during the long, painful night hours was finally finished. He knew he could never escape the rebels. But tonight, he would set the boat free.

He limped down to where the waves hissed up onto the shore, and saw the calm stretch where he knew there was a dangerous rip, sucking the water out to the Atlantic Ocean. He was about to set the boat upon its journey, when he stopped suddenly.

As the moonlight cast an eerie glow on the waves and the beach, Sambula thought about what he most wanted. The crackle of gunfire, closer this time, floated over the waves. He missed his grandfather and he missed his peaceful life back in the village. He carefully cradled the boat in his hand and carved the words "go in peace" onto its deck before lowering it into the dark water.

The incredible journey had begun.

2 Fifteen Years Later ...

Wise tourists and wealthy foreigners never ventured this far south. By mid-morning, the beautiful Brazilian beaches to the north were full of smiling holidaymakers, the smell of suntan oil and the beat of popular Latin music.

But here, where Luiz sat on an upturned oil drum staring out to sea, there was nothing attractive – only run-down shacks, hungry people with no work, and streets backing onto the filthy, oil-stained beach. This was a shanty town. Crime was everywhere and life here was dangerous.

In the past year, Luiz had spent a lot of time being angry. He was angry at the world. He was angry with the people in it, especially the rich tourists who spent more money in a week than he could earn in a lifetime. But he was most angry with his father, for leaving him on his own.

Being deserted was something Luiz would never get over.

Suddenly, his eye caught sight of something among the rubbish that coated the beach. Carefully, he edged his way down to the filthy sand and reached out.

He couldn't believe his eyes.

It was a small, carved wooden boat with something written on it. Luiz narrowed his eyes, and looked around. No-one else was there. He pocketed the boat and clambered back up to the oil drum. Maybe he'd be able to sell the toy for a few coins. After a night without food, he was starving. A few coins would go towards buying him some bread, at least.

Then, just as Luiz was about to head back into the mean streets and alleyways of the shanty-town, he spotted the tourist. He looked lost and nervous. This was too good to be true!

Luiz silently crept up behind the unfortunate tourist, who was anxiously looking at a map.

Luiz could see a wad of dollar notes in the man's back pocket.

"Just one," thought Luiz, narrowing his eyes. He reached out, and –

Suddenly, the tourist whirled around, sensing danger. Luiz snatched a green American dollar note from the man's pocket, spun on his heels, and blindly raced towards the nearest alleyway. Too late, he saw the blue and white uniform turning the corner and within a split-second, his shoulder was in the painful, vice-like grip of the policeman's hand.

"You shanty-town thief!" bellowed the policeman angrily. "I'll show you what happens to thieves on my street!"

The tourist ran up to where Luiz was squirming in pain, and looked at the ragged street kid. He noticed the toy boat in the boy's pocket. Luiz looked desperately at the tourist, and for a moment, their eyes connected. Then the tourist spoke to the policeman.

"He didn't steal anything," said the tourist. "I gave him the dollar."

Luiz stared in disbelief at the tourist, who kept his eyes firmly fixed on the policeman's face. "I gave him the dollar," he repeated. "I was buying a souvenir toy boat. Let him go."

The policeman reluctantly released his tight grip and Luiz scrambled free. He stared at the stranger. He was about to get a much-needed second chance.

"Thank you," Luiz gasped. Then he turned and fled down a dark shanty-town alley.

3 Fifteen Years Later ...

Rihanna knew that her dad was coming home. Her mother was fussing around their San Diego apartment, tidying everything, making it spotless, just in time for Rihanna's dad's return.

Rihanna's dad travelled a lot for his job. He always seemed to be away, or delayed at airports, or on important business in places Rihanna had never heard of. Rihanna talked to her father more on the phone than in person.

It seemed like every phone call was the same.

"Got to go," her dad would say. "They're calling my flight."

"I love you, Dad," Rihanna would reply. But usually the connection was already dead.

Rihanna watched her mum rearranging the cushions on the couch.

"Will he be able to come to my school prize-giving?" she asked. "It's tomorrow night."

"Maybe," replied her mother, biting her lip. "We'll see."

Rihanna's father always made a grand entrance. Whenever she saw his beaming smile and heard his laughing voice, Rihanna knew why he was always travelling. Everyone liked her father and they liked doing business with him. But she just wished they would share him with his family a little more.

After her mum and dad had kissed, he dropped his suitcases on the floor. "Where's my favourite girl?" he said, with a broad smile and open arms. Rihanna grinned shyly. It always felt a little strange seeing her dad again. A month away was a long time.

"Hi Dad," she smiled, giving him a big hug.

"I've got so much to tell you both," said her father.

"But first, I think I've got a little something for my girl. Now where did I put it?"

Rihanna smiled. Her dad did this every time. He'd bring her a present from wherever he'd been and pretend he'd forgotten where he'd put it.

"Ah!" he announced with a wink. He pulled a small gift box out of his cabin bag. "I wonder what this is?"

Rihanna was just glad to have her father home – but she went along with his game all the same. She slowly unwrapped the gift, and gasped when she saw the beautifully carved boat. Her fingers traced some words carved into its deck.

"Go in peace", she read. Beneath, in worn lettering, was written "Learn forgiveness".

"When I was in Brazil last week, I bought it from a charity that runs schools for homeless kids," explained her father. "Luiz, the guy who runs it, told me that all the money goes towards helping children from the poorest areas attend school."

"That's nice, dear," said Rihanna's mother. "And speaking of school, Rihanna's got something to ask. Haven't you, darling?"

Rihanna smiled and gazed up at her father. "I was just wondering if you could come to my prize-giving tomorrow," she said excitedly. "It'll be really cool – I've done really well at maths, and I might even get a prize."

Suddenly, her father's face looked vague and his eyes looked away from Rihanna's.

"Hey, that's a wonderful idea," he said, looking at his wife. "And you know I'd really love to, but I've got some really fantastic news of my own."

Rihanna smiled, hoping that her expression would hide her disappointment.

"What's that, dear?" asked her mother.

"I've been promoted," said Rihanna's father. "I'm now vice-president in charge of Europe, as well as North and South America. Isn't that just great?"

"That's wonderful," replied Rihanna's mother.

Rihanna's father beamed again, but there was something in her mother's voice and smile that sounded strained.

"It means I'm flying to Paris tomorrow," said her father cheerily. "Another twelve-hour flight, another airport, another hotel room. But think of the presents I'll be able to buy my two favourite girls in those French boutiques!"

Rihanna wanted to tell her father it wasn't presents she wanted. It was him. But she didn't.

Later that week, Rihanna caught the bus down to the beach. She wore the trendy leather sandals her dad had brought back one time from New York. Over her shoulder, she carried a designer bag that he had brought her from Argentina last month. In her bag was the small boat he'd bought her from Brazil. She'd added her own message, carved with a souvenir nail file that he'd brought her from Mexico.

She watched families stroll along the boardwalk and wondered what it was like in Paris.

"Got to go," were the last words her father had said to her on the phone before he left.

Rihanna walked down to the edge of the blue Pacific Ocean and curled her toes into the soft, warm sand.

"I love you, Dad," she had replied. But it was too late. The connection was dead.

Rihanna walked down to the edge of the ocean. She put the little boat in the water and watched it float away.

4 Fifteen Years Later ...

Work on the Australian prawn boats was rough and dangerous, but the money was good – if you survived.

Off the north-eastern coast, cyclones tore across the Coral Sea with a fury that could sweep even the best deckhand overboard.

Mandawuy's eyes and hands stung. He felt miserable. The salt from the seawater blurred his vision, and seemed to eat painfully into the cuts and blisters on his hands. This was a bad voyage. There'd been few prawns and a lot of bad weather.

"This is the last time," Mandawuy had promised himself. Just like the last voyage – and the one before that.

The captain sounded a warning blast on the siren and the giant mechanical winch on deck ground into action, hauling the huge nets onboard.

Mandawuy stared at the choppy ocean, hoping that this net would be full. A full net would mean a good payday. But he was disappointed.

The net swung overhead, and Mandawuy pulled the rope to release its contents. A few prawns fell onto the sorting table. There was a lot of seaweed and driftwood. With a practised arm, Mandawuy swept the prawns into a chute that led to the hold, and gathered up the weed and wood to throw overboard.

Then something caught his eye. Among the flotsam that the net had hauled onboard was a small carved boat. Mandawuy looked again, and picked out the small piece of wood.

Suddenly, a huge wave crashed over the deck and Mandawuy braced himself for the rush of water. He slipped the small carved boat into his fluorescent orange deckhand's jacket, and held on tight.

"This is the last time," he said, between gritted teeth, as the spray filled his eyes, mouth and nostrils.

Back on shore, the fishing company had a handful of scrawled messages waiting for him.

"Call home, urgent!" they all said. Mandawuy sighed. His family lived on the other side of Australia and messages like that usually meant they needed money. Unfortunately, he had more messages than money after this terrible voyage.

He walked dejectedly up the wharf and found a payphone. He dialled the number and waited. As soon as his aunty answered, he could tell that something was wrong.

That night, Mandawuy sat on his bed in the deckhand's quarters, shaking his head. He couldn't believe that his brother was dead – killed by a drunk driver.

"You are the eldest now, Mandawuy," his aunty had pleaded. "You must come home. Your family needs you."

But Mandawuy didn't want to go home. He hated the hot, dusty town where there was nothing to do, no future and too much crime.

He stared at the fluorescent-orange deckhand's jacket hanging from the hook on the back of his door. Even though he'd said "this is the last time," he wondered how soon he could get back on board.

Then he remembered the boat he had found.

He reached into the jacket pocket and pulled out the damp piece of carved wood.

There were three lines, carved in different lettering underneath each other.

"Go in peace. Learn forgiveness. Share love."

Mandawuy sat on the edge of his bed, thinking about his brother, and the hot, dusty town where his family waited. And he knew what he had to do.

Go in Peace
Learn forgiveness
Share love

Twelve months later, Mandawuy looked at the main street of his hometown, filled with red dust and stunted saltweeds. A pack of yellow dogs stared back at him from the shade of a gnarled tree. A few kilometres beyond, the bright blue of the Indian Ocean shone like a huge, rippling sapphire. On the surface, nothing much had changed since he'd left all those years ago.

But a year spent travelling westwards had changed Mandawuy – and the lives of those people he had come into contact with.

Across the northernmost part of Australia, he'd walked; caught lifts with truck drivers; walked again; ridden a cattle owner's horses; walked again; and at every stop, Mandawuy spread his message.

His one-man campaign against dangerous driving had even been on the TV news.

"One man walking across Australia, making a difference!" the newsreader had said.

But Mandawuy hadn't seen the report. He'd been in a small town with no TVs, speaking at a town meeting. And now he was in another small town.

A door opened, and a familiar face peered out.

"I knew you'd come back," said his aunty. "You being home will make all the difference."

"You're right, aunty," nodded Mandawuy. "I will make a difference."

A month later, Mandawuy allowed himself an hour out of his busy schedule to have some time on his own.

He walked along the beautiful beach and watched an amazing sunset hover above the shimmering horizon of the Indian Ocean.

He was due to catch a small plane down to Perth, where he was speaking at a national conference on health and safety education – but first, he had something to do.

He walked down to the waterline and bent down. He released a small carved boat into the Indian Ocean, to which he'd added his own line.

"Travel well," he said. "Find your way home."

5 Fifteen Years Later ...

The old man felt tired. The heat from the African sun warmed his ancient bones, and the sunlight made his eyes water. But it was still his favourite spot, sitting on the ocean shore, looking eastwards, out to sea.

"Will there be anything else, Mr President?" asked the nurse who was rearranging the blankets on his wheelchair.

"I'm fine," smiled the president. "Go now."

The president closed his eyes and listened to the sounds of the tropical birds, the waves, and the laughter coming from the busy village behind him. How different it had been when he had first come here.

He watched the waves rolling in and thought about the many things he had achieved. He no longer did much, except make a few speeches of course – the younger men and women in the government had much more energy. But they all respected him and drew upon his wisdom.

Suddenly, the president noticed something sweep up onto the shore. His pale, watery eyes fixed upon the tiny object, and an old, half-forgotten memory began to stir.

The waves pushed the object further up the shore, closer to the wheelchair.

The president reached for his stick and heaved himself up out of the chair. He didn't really need it, he told himself. It was just that his left leg was playing up again. That dull ache. In all those years, no doctor had been able to stop it.

The small object floated closer, and the president reached down.

It couldn't be, of course. That would be impossible. But it did look very familiar.

The president slumped back into the wheelchair and slipped out his reading glasses. He turned the small piece of wood over and over, and looked in amazement at the smooth, faded words carved into it.

GO IN PEACE
LEARN FORGIVENESS
SHARE LOVE
STAND TALL

The President smiled, and as he held tightly to the small boat, he closed his eyes for the last time.

When the nurse found him later that afternoon, he still had a smile on his face.

The passing of their beloved president caused great sadness in the African country. The peace and wisdom he had brought to his people had changed many lives – and the messages he had inspired had touched many more around the world.

“Go in peace. Learn forgiveness. Share love. Stand tall.”

There could be no better memory of President Sambula.

THE END